TRAILER PARK ELEGY

TRAILER PARK ELEGY

Cornelia Hoogland

HARBOUR PUBLISHING

Harbour Publishing Co. Ltd.
P.O. Box 219, Madeira Park, BC, V0N 2H0
www.harbourpublishing.com

Cover design by Anna Comfort O'Keeffe
Cover image by Michael Spear / Stocksy
Text design by Mary White
Printed and bound in Canada

Harbour Publishing acknowledges the support of the Canada Council
for the Arts, which last year invested $153 million to bring the arts to
Canadians throughout the country. We also gratefully acknowledge
financial support from the Government of Canada and from the
Province of British Columbia through the BC Arts Council and the
Book Publishing Tax Credit.

Library and Archives Canada Cataloguing in Publication

Hoogland, Cornelia, author
    Trailer park elegy / Cornelia Hoogland.

Poems.
Issued in print and electronic formats.
ISBN 978-1-55017-815-9 (softcover).—ISBN 978-1-55017-816-6
(HTML)

    I. Title.

PS8565.O6515T73 2017   C811'.54   C2017-902937-1
                                            C2017-902938-X

For Lynn Casey

You are neither here nor there,
A hurry through which known and strange things pass
As big soft buffetings come at the car sideways
And catch the heart off guard and blow it open.

—Seamus Heaney

Table of Contents

Put the car in park,   11

And the next day   12

Deep Bay opening   13

Where my brother came when he got out of rehab. Halfway   14

Hey. From this one syllable   15

My niece leaned against the rail, laughing.   16

No! erupts from my tea thermos   17

Weather brief: Hwy 37N—   18

Highway 37N rose from the sea.   19

The road builders arrived: 20

The ice   21

Can you get me out of here?   22

Humans draw 14,000 breaths   23

Like the scene in *Beowulf*—   24

Inside my car nothing moves. *Still Life with Air Bag.*   25

Between Angel station and King's Cross   26

I was   28

Too late now. Tide   29

A photo tumbles from the maps.   30

Did his life flash before him,   31

Did he revisit his school playground,   32

The little room   33

We shared bad knees. *Both knees,* he said   34

You were always the best news.   35

Because a bus   36

When the sound hit the tympanic bone,
    the thin tympanic plate,   37

When it hits me.   38

The dog checks   39

At the entrance to the trailer park,   40

What did Tecumseh mean when he said,   41

When did night fall? Dark early, these days.   42

My brother alone in his boat   43

Gust of wind catches the car door.   44

Clear ice, rime. Long freeze, deep   45

Breeze gathered the bedsheets   46

Chin hooked over the front seat, my eyes   47

His absence is a room   48

The first thing she sees when she comes home   49

To see our marbled planet from space,   50

He left Dease Lake as the sky was lifting.   51

Driving around Vancouver with my brother,   52

A friend asks, were you close?   53

And this: the set of his mouth,   54

The rising sun hits my Toyota's back window, the interior,   55

I grew up next to a graveyard   56

Umbrellas snap shut, people   57

The box. Gargoyle   58

Like the fainting game   59

I hear *spindle*   60

Now I skip stones.   61

If you can, return   62

Waves, not exactly uniform   63

My heart is under   64

I dreamt a wild animal   65

Now we sort out what's his.   66

Hot-air lanterns release   67

I've been reading how dark matter—invisible antimatter,   68

Closing up Deep Bay that last winter.   69

Watch, he said, hiding the key.   70

Because the moon has no atmosphere, it can't scatter   71

A 26-pound spring Mom's reeling in   72

Little brat, running   73

Salamander in his boy hand,   74

To the dog's keen nose you're here   75

More clearly now than ever, light separates
     into distinct zones.   76

Inside my brother's truck—   77

And here's my rusting car   78

World like a shelter   79

World like a cold front,   80

The dog's wet nose pokes the air.   82

I'm the sibling who travelled to the other   83

Roll down the car window—   84

Is it wind   85

Endnotes   86

Acknowledgements   87

About Cornelia Hoogland   88

≈≈≈

Put the car in park,
the engine sputters. Dies.

        Beyond
the red hood of my Toyota,
under maples, a row of mobile homes
curves round a stone beach.

Rusty leaves fly into vinyl siding,
rattle at RV windows. Nobody's home.
The park is deserted.

        The sea is deserted.

At the horizon, fold where
sky and water meet, the membrane
between the living and the dead
        thins.

I shift in my seat, listen
to an outboard motor diminish,
        reverberate,

that half-life between sound
and memory of sound.

≈≈≈

And the next day
and the next—
parked in the visitors' lot
at the locked gate.

Wind frets the bungied tarps
covering the summer furniture.

        Dog with me,
walking the shoreline in gale,
slant rain striking our faces.
Above the swells, the gulls
are sharply drawn.
They look down. Darkness

        leaks from their wing tips.

≈≈≈

Deep Bay opening
the mouths of the dead.

≈≈≈

Where my brother came when he got out of rehab. Halfway
down Gainsberg Road, right at the shake house weathered grey,
wide view of the bay.

He climbed the rise. The ocean, the air, his own depth.
Couldn't speak—
stood staring and breathing.

Mt. Baker's snow-summit—afloat in a cumulus sea—will sometimes
present its shining self. But the gift was breath—he didn't know
his own would make him cry.

Did musicians regret the end of vinyl, and the halfway pause plotted
into their albums for turning the record,
starting the second side?

My brother's second side, three sober years—were gravy, pure
gravy.

≈≈≈

Hey. From this one syllable
I was to discern whose voice
was on the other end of the phone.
Then the deluge—detail on detail
'til my ear was cauliflower.
He had more characters than Dickens,
and I got to know them:
Nurse Ratched at rehab,
Eddy the knife collector, fish stories
in Skinny Al's tremulous voice.
Funny. My brother the butt
of his own story, the fall guy.
He wasn't always, he became that;
man who knew *he* was the punchline.
              No, wait, it gets better.

≈≈≈

My niece leaned against the rail, laughing.
A barbeque, a sweet September night.

My brother and his wife drove home
along the coast through Courtenay,
Royston, both bays—Union and Fanny—
turned off at the fire hall down the twisting hill
to Deep Bay, RVs bordering the ocean.
Plaster gnomes on the lawns, *Children Playing* sign,
a sodium moon over the public washroom.

The next day he travelled 1000 kilometres
NW of Vancouver to Dease Lake,
where he supervised concrete pours
into a run-of-river hydroelectric dam.

On that last night I imagine my brother
and his wife hand in hand from the truck
to the sliding glass doors of the cabana
where they removed their shoes like children
and climbed the stairs to bed and held each other.

≈≈≈

No! erupts from my tea thermos
when I loosen the stopper.

Like a Greek chorus, voices cry:
Don't let go! Hold tight
each mammalian comfort!

Chorus old as fish trap,
as midden, as our species.

    A wail lifts
rocks from the beach,
bellows the sand,
the bay.

≈≈≈

Weather brief: Hwy 37N—
compact snow with slippery sections
from junction Hwy 16 @ Kitwanga to
Cranberry River, 76 kms north.

≈≈≈

Highway 37N rose from the sea.
For eons the road bed was underwater,
carried north on the Pacific Ocean floor.
Slivers of iron ran through it, yearning
for the North Pole. The rocky mass
never got there, thrust instead 85 metres
above sea level, listing eastward.

≈≈≈

The road builders arrived:
heavy equipment for the
cut slope, fill slope,
the rough grade,
the surface.

But no, none of these
were responsible.
No rupture, scarred geology.
No tectonic plates—
continent-sized scapula—
colliding. No fault
line.

      Just a wrinkle
      in the road.

≈≈≈

The ice

was invisible.
The pavement unexceptional.

Black ice and nothing could keep his tires on the road.

≈≈≈

Can you get me out of here?

Eric—the man who stopped at the side of the highway
where my brother lay dying—peered
into the dim truck cab.

Are you alone?

Yes ...

I'll get you out, said Eric. *Help is on the way.*

... Thank you ...

≈≈≈

Humans draw 14,000 breaths
a day. What is spoken

is spoken on the exiting
breath. Our meanings,

an entire life's meaning,
              Thank you,

can ride the exhale.

≈≈≈

Like the scene in *Beowulf*—
warriors in the mead hall; late night.
Fire in the hearth, dogs beneath
the table. Laughter.

Above the revellers, a sparrow
from out of the dark flies in through a window,

crosses the length of the lit hall,

exits.

≈≈≈

Inside my car nothing moves. *Still Life with Air Bag.*

I rifle through the glove compartment.
Bulky maps. Unfold a dated *TTC* brochure,
trace the lozenge-shaped subway line
from Union Station to Spadina. Run my finger over
Bloor's blue line of shops; that great coffee.

I try to refold the map.

≈≈≈

Between Angel station and King's Cross
the tube thundered under the ground
of the flat I rented in Islington.
Every half-hour it rattled
me, then became me.

        The sound
of the rise and boom of the beach
against my car windows.
I press my hand to the glass.

A whale in its depth, echoing
and speaking its language.
One mammal's meaning and despair.
You can hear them on YouTube,
one orca to another, across great distances.

I hear my brother—

(shouting) *I never know what city you're in.*
Never know where you are. Where are you?

≈≈≈

I was
on a fast track, on
my motivated way
            somewhere.

Bristling metals.

Sky Train. Subway. Autobahn. Metro. Tube.

Because we're all speeding
east or west in our little vehicles,
in the dashboard's glow,
pitching who knows where.

I heard his suffering.
I drove harder, faster.

≈≈≈

Too late now. Tide
returns, floods
into Deep Bay,
        ebbs into the Pacific,
        widening, spreading.

I slump into the steering wheel.

I see now
it's not his—
this darkness

        that split open

at his death.

It's mine. Always has been.

≈≈≈

A photo tumbles from the maps.
Light from a dead star
streams past my brother.

He looks chilled. His lips
part. He exhales.
He hollows for flight.

Always the sparrow of fear—
wing-flutter in the middle of the hall
where air currents collide.

He wears sunglasses.
There's a baby in his arms.
Her tiny palm on his chest.

She has the look of the newly arrived—
recently from that world
to which my brother is going.

≈≈≈

Did his life flash before him,
a kind of holographic rewind?
Did he orbit his first apartment
on McBride in New West,
peer through the windows,
catch glimpses of himself

on the seventh floor, say, cooking
macaroni, the cheese-powder lending
an even, orange wash to the room?
At the table, his three children, knives
and forks upright in their small fists.

Did 3-D sound embellish each scene?
Distant traffic on the Trans-Canada,
a kitchen chair being pushed across a floor,
and under his shirt his heart banging on.

I imagine one room lighting up
a list of questions he would've asked
before leaving the world;

a flash in another—
and he could've watched himself
get out of bed, feel his way
downstairs where his computer
was updating Office 12.2.3.

The apartment sways, leans a little.
A black, swirling dress. Dark spaces between
the trees at the end of the cul-de-sac.
At a basement window, up against glass,
a chain of paper dolls hold hands.

≈≈≈

Did he revisit his school playground,
that towering slide? His shoes clanking
on the metal rungs as he climbed his way,
through hesitations, to the top.

I trust Eric's report of my brother's last words.
They match his pleasures in turning a salmon
on the barbeque, hauling up prawn traps
as the sun set over the Beaufort Range.
He let the boat drift, caught the rope
he yarded and coiled onto the floor boards.
As the trap, heavy with prawn, neared
the surface, my brother pointed to tiny pink
crabs that clung to the ascending rope,
now jumping like fleas to the dark.

My brother's satisfaction, at the end of fear,
of surviving the hundred-faced bully.

What he had to say for himself was *thank you.*

≈≈≈

The little room
of my car, within
            the drip-line
            of firs.

Plunk   *I*

Plunk   *am*

Plunk   *here*

I run my hand over the plastic
cup holder, storage cubbies in the dash, ashtray
sliding open. Spare change.

Here. Now I'm here.

≈≈≈

We shared bad knees. *Both knees,* he said
to his doctor, *do them both.* Now it's my turn,
I'm wheeled into the operating room, cold,
I'm thinking ligaments, torn meniscus,
nerves like fingers, signalling. My insides,
obscure as caves and ocean floors, the long arms
of galaxies we're swirling in. Those, together
with tables, chairs and observable phenomena,
are a puny 4% of the total mass of the universe.
And here's the kicker: the remaining
96% of the material world is invisible dark matter.
The doctor asks if I'd like to watch the procedure
on a screen. You'd think I'd grab the chance.
My insides revealed, view magnified.
Turns out I want to rest my head
on the pillow and stare at the green ceiling.
That's when "Just Breathe" by Pearl Jam
comes on the radio. *Huh? You? Here?*
I laugh, can't help it, it's crazy.
The doctor scowls. A nurse hands me
a Kleenex, points to my eyes. My brother,
I want to explain, post knee surgery,
dripping sweat as he crab-walked
on his hands   over the floor
in that time we were both alive.

≈≈≈

You were always the best news.

When you pulled into the driveway,
opened the truck door—
my dog went nuts
grinning and batting his tail.

I'm not saying this in the right order.

The salt air, the mock orange
belongs to the fifty-acre
Bowen Park. *Our woods, brother.*

Something catches—

                    (a butterfly
closes her wings

≈≈≈

Because a bus
at high speed in white space.
Because a Sky Train. Freeway. Autobahn.
Rubber tires whump over asphalt.

We think the Strait of Georgia is silent
when really it's roaring.

A barge. A container ship—
blistering furnace from China—
squeezes its hulk
through Seymour Narrows.
Cargo on its way to box stores.
On the deck sky-high cranes,
a dozen semi-trailers.
Blue polyprop rope.

Because
        a tiny deviation in the ship's
bank of diesel engines. The slightest
fraction of a degree
        off course—

        the steel hull shears
Quadra Island's bedrock.

The only sound above
is waves, shocked and leaping high
up Quadra's cliffs.

But under water a decibel roar
travels its warped, bent path—

≈≈≈

When the sound hit the tympanic bone, the thin tympanic plate,
when the pressure levels (chronic at 202 dB re1µPa2s) accelerate
as tanker traffic and seismic surveys increase, when ocean basins
reverberate explosions detonated every ten seconds over
months, when shipping traffic doubles each decade,

    it degrades the underwater acoustics, masks
    the low-frequency whale speech,
    interferes with echolocation
    among the transient orcas
    that migrate in late winter
    through the southern end
    of the Salish Sea for
    the return of herring,
    the Gulf Islands
    thick with tankers
    crowding the
    already-
    crowded
    narrows.

≈≈≈

When it hits me.
When I hear.
When the field of his death
becomes my field—
something touches me,
back of the knee.

My dog, leash
between his teeth.

I follow him
to the beach, glad
to be tethered.

≈≈≈

The dog checks
I'm with him,
keeps a distance between us.

        His backside's
satisfying, like horses
in old cowboy movies,
reins looped over the rail
in front of the saloon.

≈≈≈

At the entrance to the trailer park,
a wooden house pole, a Watchman.

Six feet tall, charred and roughly
carved, head tilted upward.
Who is this rooted character
                    facing outward?

The worst has already happened.
He has all the time there is.

≈≈≈

What did Tecumseh mean when he said,
You have all the time there is?
He was speaking to English generals,
to Brock; it was 1812, the war on.

On tidal flats, shifting sand, is time water,
now liquid, now frozen, now falling?
Cycles, seasons, geology? Can time fix
into place, seal at the edges, become memory?
Can time be lost? My body a container
of loss? Memory embedded in my tissue
like trauma or fat; now excavated, retrieved?

                Not even a writer
alone on the edge of the sea is enough
removed. I speak in dashes
                    water closes over
with a clap. Beach logs rush in with the storm.

≈≈≈

When did night fall? Dark early, these days.
A low sky goes purple-black. Cold
weather settles in, October rain
smacks the windshield. Smell of wet dog,
soggy car mats. Rain's tempo surges
. and slurs in overlapping rhythms.

In a flash of lightning, the far end
of the bay switches on like streetlights.
Roiling amber-green waves frozen
at break-point. As suddenly
switches off. Black again. Nothing.

But a nothing-charged-with-absence.
The briefly illumined mead hall, life's
swift transit *Beowulf*'s sparrow
might have sensed leaving the light
behind.

≈≈≈

My brother alone in his boat
on black water in rain.

Air's small, damp fingers.

≈≈≈

Gust of wind catches the car door.
The dog, wild for Deep Bay, jumps out,
digs his nose into a fermenting carcass
on the beach, trots to the weir—an intertidal
fish trap built by the Pentlach people.

2000 years later, the moon still tugs
the sea to the edge. Pulls
it over the rock necklace
into the catchment pool.

And now the scene includes
the steady light of the station
on Chrome Island,
the Coastguard-white buildings;
their steeply pointed roofs
                    sliding into the sea.

≈≈≈

Clear ice, rime. Long freeze, deep
freeze. Frost, northern lights.
frozen rinks, the Rideau Canal.

Before 1962, black ice
didn't exist. Historically unknown
to the Innu, expert
cataloguers of ice and snow.

Then: asphalt,
highways and speeds over 60,
just-in-time delivery—
401 Detroit-to-Toronto.

The year my brother turned four,
the TV newscaster, warning *invisible, deadly,*
shaped his lips around
the freshly minted term, *black ice.*

≈≈≈

Breeze gathered the bedsheets
Mother pinned to the clothesline. Billowed
them sky-high as crow's nest on ship's mainmast:
the wet flapping wonders of the world.
On the grass beneath we set sail.

≈≈≈

Chin hooked over the front seat, my eyes
      on a road that spooled us
      like a blow-up party favour.

Dad's hands on the wheel of his sky-blue Comet,
Mom in the passenger seat, my baby brother on her lap.

The road's parallel lines rush at her, pull her

      into the arc of a story
      she'll spend years telling, about her friend
      whose husband, then son, died.
      It's one thing to lose your husband—

            but to lose a son—
            slow shake of her head, side to side.

      The vanishing point
      Mom rehearsed so often it became
      her story
      her road.

≈≈≈

His absence is a room

she walks into.

Every

day.

≈≈≈

The first thing she sees when she comes home
from shopping is an oversize photo
of her son. Since my brother died she is in
constant conversation. *Hello! I'm back.*
Leans her cane against the dining room table,
unpacks her bargains, recites both regular
and sale price, tallies up her savings.
Says: good morning, good night,
the weatherman forecasts snow,
her knees (she pats the left) acting up
as the barometer rises. The ducks
at the sliding glass doors need to be fed,
the widow across the lane may be lonely.
She works at being cheerful.
Tells herself he's safe now, dry and warm.
Searches the photo for two white squares,
the catchlight of each iris.

≈≈≈

To see our marbled planet from space,
you'd never guess the tiny dramas,
the human family in masquerade: polished
Sunday shoes, starched dress, a boy-sized suit.
Backstage, we six immigrants awaiting our cues
never broke silence. We still don't

but him!

His last three yakkety years he spilled
the beans. Oh, the beans, the split-
open jar exploding the permissible
thickness of peanut butter
on a slice of toast; the *Father* and *Son*
of the Holy Trinity teaming up
with Maple Leafs' Johnny Bower as *Goalie Host*.
My brother played our dour lives for laughs,
parodied Dad's *This is what we do.*
Cozied up to religious feeling then
stoned with punchlines. When he was
a kid, it was the wise crack
delivered under his breath. His death-
defying human freefalls
in the face of *Because I said so.*
Whenever he dropped little depth-charges
I reverted to being an anxious child. Had to
remind myself he was not twelve, but fifty—

my brother talking, telling, saying who he was.

≈≈≈

He left Dease Lake as the sky was lifting.
When he fed the key into the lock
and the company-truck door swung, like day
on its hinge, was there a sign?
The geese sculling north, honking as they flew?

I imagine him tossing his carry-on into the cab,
sliding his hips into the driver's seat, sunglasses on the dash.
Cellphone on the console.

He leaned back, exhaling as he pushed the palms of his hands
over his thighs. (I don't need *hands* in that last sentence
but I want them.) Key in the ignition, vehicle
onto the highway, to the airport and home.

His last hours on earth.

I keep returning to that cab, fondling every minute
of his last minutes, dividing them into two, into six, into sixty.

His phone was out of range.
Sometimes in the night
I hear it ringing.

≈≈≈

Driving around Vancouver with my brother,
shopping for ceramic tile at swishy stores
like Tierra Sol. Charcoal grey tile, tile
the red of baked earth. We narrowed the choice
to *Florim Ethos* and the deeper *Turbostone*—
but I'd already chosen a serviceable grey
at Tile Mart. It was never about the tile.

It was about him—what was difficult,
what came easily. His body.
He owned his legs and arms, his head
philosophical on his shoulders.
It turned this way and that. I wanted

what it saw. Cyclists, clacking horns,
puddles banking up from delivery vans.
Behind a chain-link fence a building
emerged from the ground, a job he'd supervised.
Accomplishments, things he was proud of.

He cranked the window, switched off the radio.

We drove in cobbled silence.
The truck cab, a cocoon.
We were pupae, listening.
We might grow wings or
                    never emerge.

≈≈≈

A friend asks, were you close?
When I say yes, this is what I mean:

I'm in the kitchen, fixing drinks.
My family's on the lawn under the Garry oaks.
I can't hear what my brother says
as he gesticulates—arms that leap
large and backlit in my memory,
in flannel sleeves, sweat and cedar,
boyhood's cut grass and almonds.

That afternoon, watching from the window,
I see reflected in my daughters' faces
the story my brother animates.
He opens his hands,
shapes a funnel his life
pours through.

≈≈≈

And this: the set of his mouth,
as if pleased with the word he found
to express himself. His upturned lips
hooking a memory? Private joke?

And this: the way his body,
like a lawn chair opening,
unfurls onto the sofa. One knee
over the other, he draws
the crossed knee close. And weaving
his fingers, thumbs pressed to chin,
he peers over, a bird at nest-edge.
And his hands, explaining. I felt more
than I listened. I could have listened
all day. Yes, this was close.

≈≈≈

The rising sun hits my Toyota's back window, the interior,
the head rest, the back of the seat, the stick shift, slowly
reveals the rear view—
brief light across its mirror—lifts

      yellow hands over the passenger seat,
      clothes me in flannel. Pyjamas.

      Thank you.

≈≈≈

I grew up next to a graveyard
where I practised death
in the weighty
silence of black limousines,
their tires rolling
through the cemetery gate
smooth as water striders.

Even the puddles squirting up from the tires said *shhhh*.

The only other sounds were umbrellas opening, hard
heels, high heels. I listened for crying.

The first time I heard a mourner wail,
the sound fell seismic—
a rock—
a thousand-metre descent—
into the No River.

       Chasm
of a woman's grief.

Once, nobody around,
I tried moaning
but it scared me.

O it's quiet. Even the rain
is hyphens.

≈≈≈

Umbrellas snap shut, people
tuck into cars that file
like black ants in procession
out the cemetery gates.
The families merge onto Bowen Road,
abandon their dead one

in a box
on a black lawn that stretches
over the graveyard hill.

What about the person
who starts breathing again
underground? In the novel I'm reading,
Victorians furnished caskets
with a string fastened
to a bell above ground.

Hinged like a praying mantis,
an earth-moving machine stalks
to the open grave, swivels
its head, its compound eyes.
Steel fore-limbs
manoeuvre under the casket,
lift, hold

over the gaping

≈≈≈

The box. Gargoyle
on each corner, arms reaching
backwards. Like toads,
they carry burdens
on their backs. Grinning.

What they know they aren't telling.
Secret buried, dirt heaped over them.
Elliptical mound of soil

shaped like an ear, cocked
to the world
              passing it by.

≈≈≈

Like the fainting game
during school recess—
one kid squeezes another
in a crushing hug.

This game is different.
I play alone in the alley
between cemetery and house.
Lie down, wiggle
a depression in the small stones
and stiffen.

Sink my eyes
into their sockets.
Will the sky to bear
down, press
the breath out of me.
My head grows light, hollow.

At the dizzy end of the exhale
my rule is—at the last
possible moment—to spit out
the one word I hear the dead whisper
in my ear. *Rope* or *cherry* or anything.

Like fishing. A live thing surfacing from the deep.

≈≈≈

I hear *spindle*
as I push all
the breath out of me.

Spindle is what
Sleeping Beauty's father
the King forbade
on pain of death.

Ordered a raging
bonfire like the one
the neighbours set
on Guy Fawkes Day.

Every spindle
in the kingdom.
Each lethal point,
flame's upward
                    rush.

In my school skirt,
on sharp rocks,
my game was life-
and-death.

≈≈≈

Now I skip stones.

At the farthest point
of a three-skip trajectory

        a word surfaces

skims the water
in reverse, hiccups
back to
me pacing the shoreline
for something to work with.

A word, unhooked,
an undersized fish

        thrashes to shore.

≈≈≈

If you can, return
to the spit, that point of land.
Breathe the licorice
smell of fennel the Chinese
planted at the turn of the century.

That's me, *btw*, far below
on the beach, searching
the insides of cockle and clam.
Sky moody as a Dutch painting,
van Ruisdael's clouds.

The last time I saw you,
you wore a shell
to resist the weather—
elastic gussets for
freedom of movement,
wind repellent,
weighing almost nothing.

          Above me,
a bird
eyes
travelling.

≈≈≈

Waves, not exactly uniform
but military in their urgency—thousands
of cresting, spittle-white epaulets.

I open the car door. The dog shoots
from the back seat, knocking me

sideways. I steady myself against
a southeasterly blowing off the water.

Salt I'll taste later, at the kitchen sink.

≈≈≈

My heart is under
the blankets; it wears a sock.
The sock is a woollen sock,
a workman's sock—
my brother's

beauty appearing,
as it does this chilly dawn—
not distant and opposite
but like he's about to
open his mouth and speak.

Migratory robins splashing
in the pond fall silent.

The dead can't appear—I know that.
Whatever comes back
comes back shrouded;
needs cocooning.

The way one thing becomes
another, like a swimmer
who walks into the ocean—

and in the moment before descent
feels underwater currents,
an eerie calm.

≈≈≈

I dreamt a wild animal
chased me.
Then it was me
watching my dog
being ripped apart.

This is how
I became the one who survived.

≈≈≈

Now we sort out what's his.
Won't be needing his big bucks
Ramset gun—high calibre, fast work,
steel into concrete—hanging
on a curved hook in the shed.

The women wash tables, wash chairs.
The men, down at the government wharf,
remove the downriggers
from the gunnels, wipe salt off the boat.
It's what we do. We're like those
wind-up radios you crank by hand
for instructions in an emergency.

The once-familiar feelings
are what we long to have
returned:
small talk over the campfire,
where to fish, how high or low the tide.

                    Stars
shine their 13 billion year old light
on us. Bats
erratic over Deep Bay;
their flight/our breathing
shallow.

This heavy lifting.

≈≈≈

Hot-air lanterns release
into the night sky. Some rise
then fall into the black water.
Some float over the Beaufort Range.
The lifting light becomes us.

Not the children
whose words—
effortless as arms—
rise as they run
after the lanterns,
waving their wrists
and shouting:

Goodbye! We love you!

≈≈≈

I've been reading how dark matter—invisible antimatter,
black holes, dwarf stars—interacts with all that happens.
Who's to say, because after my brother died, a strange thing:
a torrent of sound—like competing talk shows at full volume—
erupted from an unused radio built into a cupboard.
A crowd's roar shot through the speakers.
My niece, in the trailer with her kids, finally
located the source, but she couldn't find the switch.

I couldn't turn it off, she said, later. She laughed
but it was a nervous laugh. *I know it was him.*

≈≈≈

Closing up Deep Bay that last winter.
Watch, my brother said to his nephew, hiding
the key above the lintel.

In *The Red Book,* Jung says that the dead
assign their unfinished work
to the living. *We are lived by powers*
we pretend to understand: They arrange
our lives; it is they who direct. Auden said that.

≈≈≈

Watch, he said, hiding the key.
But I hear *listen*. I've been
leaning in—

boulders
heave their emptiness
over dune grass, crushing in their wake.

≈≈≈

Because the moon has no atmosphere, it can't scatter
the light that arrives in a single strobe from the sun.

With no illuminated sky, contrasts are severe.
His death is that incident light, the lamp

casting the world in shadow.

≈≈≈

A 26-pound spring Mom's reeling in
off Little Qualicum River. My brother's eyes are saucers.
He throttles the motor. Tiny suns bounce
off the boat boards, the waves.

I want to say to him, *Grab the rod, give Mom a hand.*
But I don't. Mom braces her legs against the gunnel,
I can feel the strength of the fish as it pulls her
into the boards. She straightens her back,
lifts her arms though it's killing her. *I'm 85 you know*,
Mom says, laughing and slackening the line.

The tension between people and fish
holds the whole thing together.
Big energy flows from my brother to Mom,
reflex runs up and down his arms.
He's poised to take over. But he doesn't.
Mom, it's your catch, your rod, you reel it in.
Even though his voice is steady and low
I know he's shouting on the inside.

A 26-pounder. Huge event, *The Big One*.

When I ask her to remember
a starring moment, this is the scene
my brother's wife reminds me of.
I need something brilliant, I'd said,
a black diamond—skiing on sun-dazzled
snow high above everything.

But no. Fish. This is him.

≈≈≈

Little brat, running
with flowers stolen
from the newly turned graves
after the cortège
slides out the cemetery gates.

Roses in particular,
cape of red
petals streaming behind you.

In the era of black and white
television, graveyard
greys, westerlies, rain—

small boy in all that colour.

≈≈≈

Salamander in his boy hand,
its chocolate skin
cold as lake water
below the raft.

≈≈≈

To the dog's keen nose you're here
in the clouds of molecules you left behind.

The Pentlach people—engineers of this fish weir
that still works—are also here. At high tide,
a ling cod gets trapped behind the boulders.

With each tidal flow—water's rush-
over-rocks—I feel the ancestors. The gravity
of stars, though it's day.

So you tug at me.

≈≈≈

More clearly now than ever, light separates into distinct zones.

Closest, on the road-side of beach logs, swathe of inky grass.

Smell of decomposing leaves. Beyond the toss-up,

sun puckers the water, narrows

the strait. Far point of land, breaking up.

≈≈≈

Inside my brother's truck—
once it stopped rolling,
and the cab groaned and the body
folded,
and the spin
          flew from the last wheel—

In the shearing,
the settling—
noise became imperceptible;
a lower frequency;
the vibration, really, of shadow
        expanding

on a solitary highway that yawned
open fields where

woods began—
and the woods

emptied on a solitary highway
      expanding

the vibration, really, of shadow,
a lower frequency;
the roar of the universe
      without us.

≈≈≈

And here's my rusting car
in a winter lot, in the clank
of flagless poles in the wind.

I breathe. There is no *I*.
I is the swinging door
between blood's metronome
and the spider web
in the bough of the Douglas fir
outside the car window.

≈≈≈

World like a shelter
the bus
late
rain
on the Plexiglas roof.

Because somewhere at high speed.
Sky Train. Subway. Autobahn. Metro. Tube.

Because we're all speeding
north or south, each in our own
little vehicle, pitching
who knows where.

Because he leaned
back in his deck chair on the patio
and fell asleep, mouth open—
and the mother bird up early fed him.

Because the newspaper fell from his hand.
Because I thought he was protected.
Rain on glass.
Rain on ice.

Because somebody said, *You better sit down,
it's your brother,* and I couldn't hear.

≈≈≈

World like a cold front,
the weather

turns. Frost
mentors the hard yellow alder

like the furzy outline
of leaves we crayoned in art class.

The shape of the heart
as we imagined it.

World like a cellphone vibrating
in a pocket. Bone

rattling bone.
World like a vandal

carving initials
in the wooden bench

at the bus shelter,
the back of the knee

where the flesh
is soft. I can't believe

the world like a shut umbrella
becomes a walking stick

brailling the sidewalk.
Reading with eyes closed

the way the blind
walk with faces tilted upward.

≈≈≈

The dog's wet nose pokes the air.

I imagine his Hubble-snout catching wind
of a dusty-rose cocoon, a nursery,
newborn stars swaddled in gauzy filaments
at the particle horizon.

≈≈≈

I'm the sibling who travelled to the other
side of the country. There's always one
who leaves home. Discontent,
desire for more, for love?
Returning, what words can I say?

I look to my scribbling hand,
the notebook on my lap,
to the empty
passenger seat, to the dog.

Know where I am, brother. Find me.

≈≈≈

Roll down the car window—
the song
of the winter wren.

The world's sorrow
is fathoms deep,
is undertow—

it shapes the darkness
that contains us.

What kind of broken are we?

        This winking
        branch-to-branch

releases into light
above the trees.

≈≈≈

Is it wind
passing through
fir needles?

What is sound
when nothing
resists it?

Deafening
container ships,
cruise liners,
screaming invasions:
sonars, seismic
air guns detonating
shock waves of noise—
obliterating

subaquatic clan-sounds,
a babbling calf
trailing its mother's
four-click morse-
code, the audio glue
of pods on the move,
on watery highways
home. A wonder
one orca
can hear another.

     Where are you?

Where are you?

Endnotes

William Jacob Martin Grootendorst was born July 9, 1958 and died on October 29, 2012. He was fifty-four years old.

Cameron Hoogland's video tribute to William Grootendorst is at: https://www.youtube.com/watch?v=M_cLCzj05Tk

For more information about the source and effect of sound pollution on whales, see "How Ocean Noise Pollution Wreaks Havoc on Marine Life," Richard Schiffman's interview with marine scientist Christopher Clark in *Yale Environment 360* (March 2016).

In a report for the World Wildlife Federation, titled "Mapping Ocean Noise: Modelling Cumulative Acoustic Energy From Shipping In British Columbia To Inform Marine Spatial Planning," Christine Erbe writes that "The noise map showed highest levels within the Straits of Georgia and Juan de Fuca, and Puget Sound, due to the location of the ports of Vancouver and Seattle." (Project CMST 1029 Report R2012-10, page i)

To credit ownership of the fish traps at Deep Bay, I depend on Tony Law's discussions with Chief Nicole Rempel of K'ómoks First Nation and Dr. Jesse Morin (archaeologist, anthropologist, and ethnohistorian), who confirmed that the title Pentlach includes K'ómoks, Sliammon and Qualicum people, all of whom have traditional interests in Deep Bay and the Comox Valley. These groups were strongly connected and shared the same language. Deep Bay is situated within the traditional unceded territory of the Pentlach people.

In the section with the first line "Where he came when he got out of rehab," I'm indebted to Raymond Carver, who famously called the last years of life "pure gravy."

In the section with the first line "We shared bad knees. *Both knees*, he said," the visible world is 4 percent of the total mass of the universe, as measured by gravity. See Richard Panek, *The 4 Percent Universe: Dark Matter, Dark Energy, and the Race to Discover the Rest of Reality*. (Houghton Mifflin Harcourt, 2011).

Acknowledgements

Thank you to the BC Arts Council, the Hornby Island Arts
Council and the Canada Council for the Arts for acknowledging
the value of my work through financial support. Also thanks
to the League of Canadian Poets and to the Writers' Union of
Canada and small reading series across the country for helping
bring these poems to audiences.

Four poems, titled *Elegy at the Trailer Park,* won second
place at the Vancouver Writers Fest, 2016. "As a Girl I Practiced
Death" was a Janet B. McCabe Poetry Prize finalist in *Ruminate.*

My deepest thanks to Ted Goodden, constant and loving
friend, my first reader. Thank you to Julie Berry, Judy LeBlanc,
Amanda Hale, Kim June Johnson, Karen Schindler, Anne
Simpson, John Donlan and Patricia Young for your generous,
valuable comments. Thank you to the wonderful people at
Harbour: Anna Comfort O'Keeffe and Emma Skagen for
overseeing this project; Nicola Goshulak; Patricia Wolfe; Mary
White; and Nathaniel Moore. Thank you, Amber McMillan,
for your encouragement. A wheelbarrow of March primula to
Traci Skuce, prized editor and writer. Thank you, Traci. To my
Cumberland and Hornby Island writing groups, sincere thanks
for your friendship. To Matt Rader who first said this was a
long poem. To Sussan Thompson and Keith Clark at Orkney
Farm, Denman Island, for Novembers on the Salish Sea. To Eric
Roy—good Samaritan, thank you. To the Gordon Webb family
at Deep Bay. To Deep Bay—the real place—where the natural
world still more or less works. Thank you to my family—each of
whom would tell this story differently.

This book is for Lynn Casey, whose generous love made all
the difference to William and continues to make the difference
to our family. For my beloved niece Alisha, nephews Jeremy and
Christopher, and their families.

And to the memory of my brother, William. *Hey.*

JENNIFER ARMSTRONG

Cornelia Hoogland's *Woods Wolf Girl* (Wolsak and Wynn, 2011) was a finalist for the Relit Award for Poetry. Her story "Sea Level" was shortlisted for the 2012 CBC Creative Nonfiction Prize. *Trailer Park Elegy* is her seventh book.

Cornelia serves on national and international literary boards, and was the founder and artistic director of *Poetry London*, and, most recently, of *Poetry* Hornby Island*, on the Gulf Island she calls home.